Stories
from
India

by
Vayu
Naidu

Illustrated by Rebecca Gryspeerdt

RSVP
RAINTREE
STECK-VAUGHN
PUBLISHERS
A Steck-Vaughn Company

Austin, Texas

www.steck-vaughn.com

OTHER MULTICULTURAL STORIES:

Stories from THE AMAZON
Stories from THE CARIBBEAN
Stories from INDIA
Stories from NATIVE NORTH AMERICA
Stories from WEST AFRICA

Published by Raintree Steck-Vaughn Publishers,
an imprint of Steck-Vaughn Company

Library of Congress Cataloging-in-Publication Data
Naidu, Vayu.
India / Vayu Naidu.
p.   cm.—(Multicultural stories)
Includes bibliographical references.
ISBN 0-7398-1335-8 (hard)
0-7398-2035-4 (soft)
1. India—Juvenile literature.
[1. India.]
I. Title. II. Series.

Printed in Italy. Bound in the United States.
1 2 3 4 5 6 7 8 9 0 04 03 02 01 00

Contents

Introduction

India is a country of many contrasts. My memory of India is mostly through sound. There are sounds of different birds in the mornings, which are then followed by the calls of different vendors: one selling vegetables, one fruits, and then one fish. Once kids are packed off to make their way to school, the office traffic begins. The sounds of different horns fill the air: cycle rickshaws, auto rickshaws, trucks, cars, motorcycles, bicycles, and carts driven by bulls and camels.

Traveling from one part of India to another, I would come across many different languages. Sometimes they shared words with my own language, and I was thrilled to be able to make out some of what people were saying. I was born and lived in New Delhi, which is in the north and is the capital of India, but my family and cultural roots are south, in Chennai. Thanks to my father and mother and their work, I traveled frequently between north and south, east and west India. On those long train journeys, in crowded compartments, I waited until stories began to emerge from people's lives, sometimes in regional languages or in different Indian English! It was my way of collecting tall tales and short stories—fat ones and long ones, too.

In this selection, I have gathered stories that are part of a living storytelling tradition. In many ways, Indians in the nuclear age live lives that parallel those of their ancestors, detailed in stories that date back earlier than the fourth century B.C. Folk tales and epics are an important part of the diet of everyone's life and are retold here.

As I have been influenced in my adult years by the south, most of these stories are set there.

Vayu Naidu

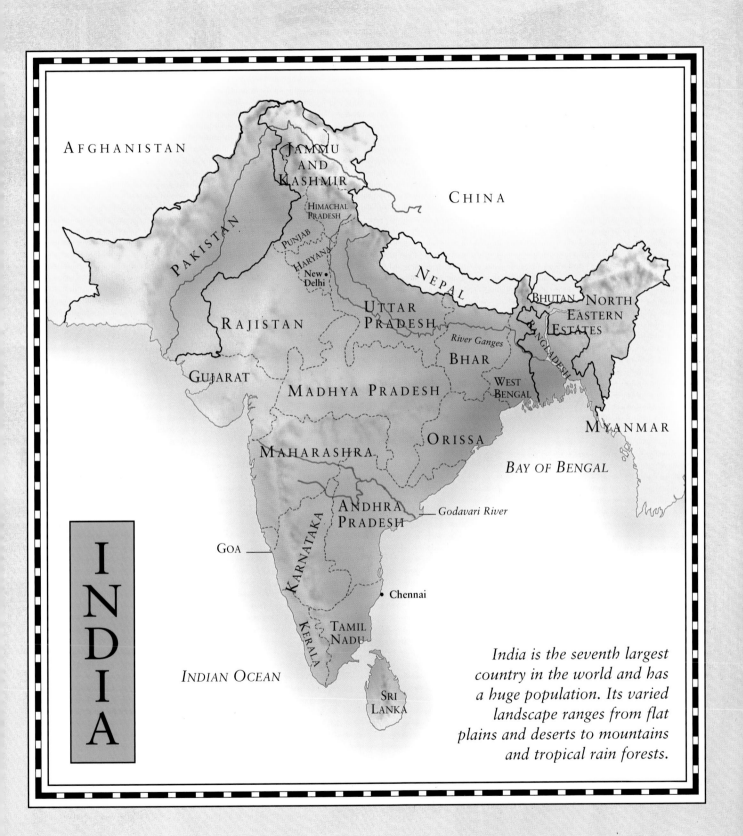

AFGHANISTAN

JAMMU AND KASHMIR

CHINA

HIMACHAL PRADESH

PAKISTAN

PUNJAB

HARYANA

New Delhi

NEPAL

BHUTAN

NORTH EASTERN ESTATES

RAJISTAN

UTTAR PRADESH

River Ganges

BANGLADESH

GUJARAT

BHAR

WEST BENGAL

MADHYA PRADESH

MYANMAR

MAHARASHRA

ORISSA

BAY OF BENGAL

ANDHRA PRADESH

Godavari River

GOA

KARNATAKA

Chennai

KERALA

TAMIL NADU

INDIAN OCEAN

SRI LANKA

INDIA

India is the seventh largest country in the world and has a huge population. Its varied landscape ranges from flat plains and deserts to mountains and tropical rain forests.

COME, LISTEN TO A STORY

There are lots of reasons why people tell stories. This special story comes within the category of "home" or "interior" folk tales, which are told when moving into a new house or at a child's cradling and naming ceremony. These kinds of stories would most often be told by elder women in the family.

This story is carried out as a form of worship in some homes in Andhra Pradesh, in southern India. Women fast and pray to Adinarayana, the sun god, so that all the members of their family may live long and well. It is a story that invites wealth and would have to be told after a ritual bath during the day.

Special occasions are times when stories are passed on. What better way to keep the storytelling tradition alive! It's true, we grow richer by feeding our imaginations, and those of our children and their children, with stories.

Andhra Pradesh has always been a storytelling center. Today, it is one of the major moviemaking states of India.

Dead Man Walking

A long time ago, there lived an old woman whose children had grown up. But still she cared for the well-being of everyone.

One day, she fasted on the seventh day of a special month. As a reward, the sun god blessed her with a story, which she had to tell someone. She ran to her sons, but they had to hurry to the king's court on business and didn't even notice her. She went to her daughter eagerly, but the daughter had a sick son to attend to. She scowled at her mother for wanting to waste time on a story. She hurried along the streets, then past the river, almost begging weavers, potters, washermen and women, but no one had the time to listen to a story.

Finally, everyone decided that the sun must have gone to her head, making her crazy. Then she saw a pregnant woman walking past. She was selling salt and looked weary. "Please," begged the old woman, "if you hear this story, you will have no misery in your life."

"All right," said the salt seller, "but I won't hear a word unless you give me some rice pudding. I'm starving."

The old woman was off in a flash to find food. But on her return it was too late. "This poor creature has fallen asleep hungry and exhausted! Oh! If only someone will hear this story, for their own good," she started wailing.

"Wait," said a voice from the salt seller's belly. "Tell me the story. I'll listen. But first, put some rice on my mother's belly button before you begin."

The old woman told her story from the sun god. She ended her tale to the unborn child, singing:

"Wherever you go, crumbling villages will become bustling towns. Cotton seeds will turn to pearls; what's more, little one, treasures will be discovered from the sea. But greatest of all, your touch will bring the dead alive!"

A few days later, the baby was born. She was a girl called Chellama. The old woman tied a sari between two banyan trees. Chellama was rocked to sleep with the birds singing the old woman's lullaby.

One day, a king came that way enchanted by the music of the birds. Then they spoke to him. "Take this child with you," they chorused. "When she is a woman, make her your wife." They sang the old woman's song. The king was delighted.

When he entered a deserted village with Chellama, suddenly there were people buying and selling juicy vegetables and fruits. Silk carpets were dusted and bought, and perfumes of all kinds wafted through the air amid carts and coaches that sped through the town.

When Chellama grew up, the king took her through his many lands filled with cotton trees. But by the next day, all these trees were laden with pearls!

After the king fulfilled the birds' prophecy and married Chellama, the first queen was naturally jealous. One day, in a fit of a temper, she decided to sink all the palace jewels in the sea. The next day the fishermen came with a huge fish. The first queen decided to send it to Chellama to have it cooked. Chellama was delighted. When she ordered it to be cut open, all the lost jewels began to pour out of the fish's belly.

"All that the birds sang about has come true," said the king when he heard the news. "But can Chellama really bring the dead back to life?" He decided to test the prophecy.

He ate the delicious fish meal at Chellama's apartments. Then he went to his first wife and, secretly, drinking poison, fell dead on her floor.

"All is gone," wailed the first wife. "Chellama, come. We must give ourselves to the funeral pyre. Get ready for Sati," she cried.

As Chellama, who was also grief stricken, began to follow her, suddenly a man whose face seemed to shine like the sun drew her aside and said: "Do as I tell you."

He bathed and told her to bathe as well. Then he told her to apply the red dot on her forehead, as he finished doing his. He told her to prepare a meal and offer it to him. Then he made her eat. When all was done according to the rites of feeding a religious man, he gave her a handful of rice, colored with turmeric.

"Scatter these grains of rice on your husband's body," he said.

"And who may you be?" Chellama asked.

"I am Adinarayana the sun god. Whoever makes the time to listen to the story of this ritual will find peace and prosperity." Smiling, he vanished.

Chellama went to the funeral pyre where the king was laid out and sprinkled the rice. To everyone's astonishment, he immediately awoke, as if from a deep sleep, and looked at all the mourners, and his first wife, wailing.

When Chellama told them what had happened, the king said: "Imagine, just by hearing that story we have seen cotton turn to pearls, fished riches from the sea, and even seen a dead king brought back to life. How much there is to gain by making the time to listen to a story!"

THE "RAMAYANA" EPIC

"Ramayana" is the oldest and most-told epic of India. Today, there are many versions of "Ramayana," and they are recited, retold, performed, danced, and adapted for television and film.

An epic is the story of a hero who has many adventures. Each adventure is a test to make him physically strong. Truth is the armor that protects him. And he offers hope and love to others around him.

One of the reasons for the popularity of "Ramayana" is its association with Diwali, the autumn festival of lights. It is a story for all ages. Often after a performance of the epic, each person in the audience is given a candy. Eating the candy after listening to the story is like tasting the story and keeping its wisdom.

The composer of "Ramayana" was transformed from a highwayman, or robber, into an epic poet.

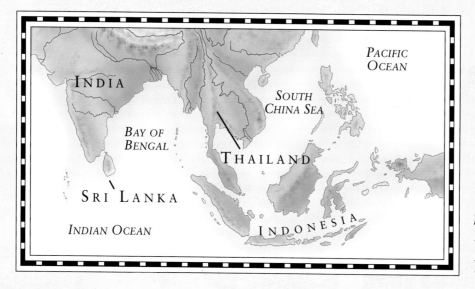

"Ramayana" is performed mainly in India, Sri Lanka, Indonesia, and Thailand.

Valmiki— the Highwayman Poet

 **I**n a deep and dark jungle, a holy man was finding a place to sit in silence. In that very jungle, there lived a daku, or highwayman, whose name was Ratnakar. He waited for travelers to pass and then he would leap at them with his spear. "That's it! You've been traveling in MY jungle. Pay up!" he would yell.

The startled travelers couldn't decide which was more frightening: his spear, his scream, or his eyes that were red and rolled like burning embers in his head.

Most people bought their lives by giving Ratnakar everything they had. The few who tried to escape fell into the pits that the daku had dug around the escape route. They would starve, and soon snakes, maggots, and other creatures tempted by rotting flesh would feast on them. Sometimes Ratnakar would see their bones shining in the moonlight and laugh to himself, thinking that he couldn't tell who might once have been fat or thin!

Of course, he had spotted the holy
man from some distance. "This must
be some procession from a temple," said
Ratnakar, "led by a holy man. Hah! If only
they knew that even the gods can't protect
them now!"

Ratnakar was grinning behind the shining blade
of his spear. Often, a procession of priests would take
the idol of worship to another village. They would be
carrying sacred vessels and jewelry that adorned the
god. "What a blessing," said Ratnakar.

The holy man came to a halt. He saw a tree offering
plenty of shade. Just as he knelt… "Stop!" screamed
Ratnakar and leaped out of the bushes with
his spear, which gleamed in the sunlight.

"Give me everything you've got,"
Ratnakar whispered menacingly as he
circled the holy man. "Otherwise, I will cut
you to pieces and throw you to the jackals."
The holy man could see by his eyes that
Ratnakar meant it, too.

"Look, my friend," said the holy man,
who was wearing a dhoti tied around his
waist to his bare feet, "do I look like
the sort of person who could possess
anything or hide anything?"

He asked in such a friendly and
musical tone that Ratnakar heard a
distant koyal replying as if it were
a call. A snake slid out to feel
more of the sound.

"Enough of your buk-buk,"
said Ratnakar between his
clenched, tobacco-stained, uneven
teeth. "You are hiding something
precious. Otherwise you wouldn't
look so calm, and I want it!"
This time he swung the spear in
the air so viciously that it made
the monkeys chatter with fright.

"Very well then," said the holy man standing and smiling. "You are right. I do have something precious. But I will only give it to you if you do something for me. Ask your family if they will die in your place and pay for all your sins. I am in no hurry to go anywhere. I will wait for your answer."

In spite of this promise, Ratnakar tied the man tightly and sped to his family, who lived camouflaged in the jungle. What a strange request, and what a price the holy man was prepared to pay for it. Or was he?

An hour later, Ratnakar returned. It was a relief that the holy man was still there, and that no animal had eaten him. Ratnakar untied him roughly, bruising him around the wrists and ankles.

"By your face I can tell no one wanted to take your place, and you have decided to leave home. Now I must keep my promise," said the holy man as he picked up a leaf.

With his thumbnail he wrote a word on the leaf, folded it, and gave it to Ratnakar. "Repeat that word with concentration. Then you will have that precious gift. Never feel that you are totally alone in life. Even if your family does not care for you, there is something within you that you can call upon," said the holy man as he turned and walked away.

Ratnakar stood dazed. He had just given up his family. He had nothing in the world. This man who had come into his life and spoke with such sweetness had changed everything. What was happening?

After some time, Ratnakar opened the leaf. The word read "maram." Ratnakar flew into a rage: "Maram! 'The world!' What good will repeating 'the world' do for me!" He spat as he uttered the word. Soon, the shadows of trees were growing long and thin. Before long, night would enter the jungle.

Ratnakar
was starving, and he decided
to kill something to eat. As he waited,
looking this way and that, he decided to repeat
the word the holy man had given him. He shut his
eyes tight and began: "Mara-mara-mara-mara-mara-
mara-mara-mara-mara…"
He soon discovered another word forming, "Rama."
As the word rolled over his tongue, he suddenly saw a
soft pink and gold light that made an arc through the
jungle. Not only that, he began to see into the
future. He saw the life of a prince named
Rama who fought against dark, evil
forces to bring light back into
the world.

Ratnakar thought: "How will I be able to share this story with anyone? I have committed so many sins. My tongue is too horrid to tell the deeds of the good Rama."

He then sat under the tree and meditated for many years on Rama. He sat so still that he didn't notice the anthills that began to form on him.

One day, he opened his eyes, and he saw two birds singing and dancing happily. Just at that moment, a hunter's arrow struck the male bird. As it fell to its death, the female bird fluttered hopelessly around.

Ratnakar cried out in pain, but the words he uttered were in verse. He sang of how joy was so abruptly put to an end without any warning. It was pure poetry. He decided to start writing the story of Prince Rama to the meter of that verse. He called it "Ramayana." It is India's first epic, and he wrote it in one hundred thousand verses.

Ratnakar came to be known as Valmiki, "the one who had such deep concentration that anthills formed on his body, and he did not know the passage of time."

Even today, his epic is recited and performed all over the world.

TENALI RAMA

Tenali Rama stories are well known in the region of Tamil Nadu, in the southeast coast of India. Stories about his wit are popular because they deal with common sense. They are the kind of "trickster" tales that enable a humble person to be wise and an apparently weak person to be strong.

Stories continue to be made up about Tenali Rama, even though there are no historical facts to tell us that what he did actually happened. The tale I've told here is inspired by his fearlessness.

Tenali Rama continues to be legendary in southern India for his wit and wisdom. When my friends and I were growing up, we used to collect Tenali Rama jokes to share at birthday parties and weddings when the grown-ups were too busy to be listening to us!

VIJAYANAGARA

Tenali Rama was a historical character in the sixteenth century, in a kingdom called Vijayanagara, which covered most of southern India.

The Goddess with Her Hands Full

In a village called Tenali, there lived a boy who was named Rama. When people passed him by, they said: "What a fine name. It's a pity he doesn't look anything like the god Rama. Instead he looks like one of those funny puppets!"

But Rama was clever and witty. He was popular among his classmates because he was absolutely fearless.

His mother used to insist that he go to the temple, but he did so only to please her. He would laugh loudly at people who visited the temples and rolled on the ground asking to be forgiven for their sins. He knew that they would go home and again do the same things they begged forgiveness for.

One day, Rama's mother insisted that he go to the temple of the goddess Kali and pray that she knock some sense into his head. He sat at the temple a long while looking at an image of the goddess Kali. She was awesome, with her dark face and large commanding eyes. She sat on a snarling tiger. She had twenty arms, and each one held a weapon to combat evil.

Suddenly Rama began laughing. He rolled on the floor and slapped it. He laughed until his sides ached, but he could not stop. Even the goddess Kali was astounded by this behavior. Normally people were very humble. In fact they bowed lower before her shrine, in comparison with what they did in front of other gods. But this boy would just not stop.

"How dare you! What do you find so funny?" she demanded as her eyes blazed, her brows knotted.

Between his bursts of laughter Rama spluttered out: "I know how great you are. But it's crazy to think you are a goddess who is so great when you have forgotten one small thing. When you have a cold, and even though you have twenty arms, you don't have a single hand free to wipe your nose. That is something you will have to beg one of us humans to do!"

Even the goddess Kali couldn't help laughing. She blessed him and foretold a prosperous career as a witty minister in the king's court. And soon he became known in history as Tenali Rama.

A TALE OF COMMON SENSE

This is a well-known tale told by religious teachers across India. It is believed that it originated with a seventh-century philosopher and Hindu saint named Sankaracharya.

He had to learn many different lessons in his life to realize that God does not sit with rich, high-and-mighty people. God is present in people who are true to themselves, and spirituality comes with following your common sense.

While Sankaracharya traveled on foot across India, he used stories to tell people about God. This tale can be read as a religious parable, but it can also be a trickster tale. There are many folk versions and mischievous ways of telling this tale. The meaning of it is simple: remember who you are and where you come from. But, most of all, follow your common sense.

INDIA

The Hindu saint Sankaracharya traveled all over India telling religious stories.

24

Folly's Wisdom

There were twelve disciples in search of Wisdom. Their leader Sowmayajulu was the thirteenth. He had told them Wisdom was to be found in a certain city in a particular kingdom. They walked all afternoon, and the sun was beating hard on their bare backs. By evening, they came to a wide river named Godavari. It was full, and the waves lapped furiously on either bank.

Sowmayajulu told his disciples: "We need to cross this river to arrive at our city of Wisdom."

The first disciple said: "Master, the river looks angry. My grandfather crossed this river once and he said she's very greedy."

"Why, what happened?" asked the second disciple.

"My grandfather was a salt trader," said the first. "He was leading a train of donkeys carrying sacks filled with salt. The river came up to the donkeys' backs. When they had crossed to the other side, they discovered that all the sacks were empty! The river was so hungry it ate up all the salt!"

The third disciple said: "Whatever shall we do? The sun is about to set, and soon it will be night. Master, command us."

Sowmayajulu looked very serious. "Hmm," his lower lip stuck out as if he were going to make an important decision. Sitting cross-legged under a tree he spoke: "Disciples, Providence has warned us about this river by that story. Let us spend the night on this bank. Early in the morning, before the sun rises, we shall see if the river is sleeping and then proceed."

The fourth disciple asked: "How do we know she is awake now?"

Some of the other disciples had started lighting a fire with branches from the tree. Sowmayajulu told the fifth disciple: "Take that branch and stick it in the water. Now!"

The disciple obeyed, as the others watched. When he stuck the burning branch in the water, it hissed. Everyone drew back. They were convinced that the Godavari River was angry.

That night some disciples slept, while others kept watch over the Godavari.

In the morning, just when the cock crowed, Sowmayajulu awoke and whispered: "Men, let's march on to Wisdom. The river must be asleep now, so we can cross."

All the willing disciples chorused: "Victory to us!"

As they began going down the sloping bank of the river, the second disciple said: "Master, how do we know the river is asleep?"

Sowmayajulu snapped a branch from a tree and plunged it into the water: "You see, have faith. This time it didn't hiss. She must be asleep. Let us cross quickly."

The Godavari River was wider than any river the disciples had ever seen. At first it was shallow, and then it was neck-deep in the middle. The twelve disciples and Sowmayajulu crossed the river as quietly as they could lest they should wake Godavari up!

When they reached the other bank, the sun was bright in the sky. Buffaloes were being driven by the villagers to graze and bask in the river. The washermen began slapping their sheets of washing on the huge black stones.

"Brothers," said the sixth disciple confidently, "now that we have reached the other bank, let me count all of us." He began, "One, two, three," and so on he went until he counted everyone except himself. "There are only twelve of us!" he cried. "Aiyiyo! That wretched river has swallowed one of our brothers up, even while she was asleep!" When the other disciples did the counting, they too came up with the same number of twelve.

They wailed so loudly that a man named Anjaneyulu, who was taking his buffalo to the river, heard them. When he saw the thirteen seekers of Wisdom weeping and rolling on the ground, he asked: "What's the matter, sirs?" When he heard what had happened, he said: "I can help you."

"Whatever price you ask of us," said Sowmayajulu, quite proud of his wealth, "we shall pay you. But get back our brother, you must!"

"Certainly," said Anjaneyulu. "Your brother will be returned to you within minutes. Follow my instructions carefully. Go to that group of cows over there and collect their dung. Bring it back here where I am standing."

The twelve disciples and Sowmayajulu left the man a sack of money that they were carrying and dashed off to gather the fresh cow dung. They gathered handfuls, even though it had an awful smell.

When they returned, Anjaneyulu said: "That's very good. Now flatten the cow dung on the path in front of you."

Once this was done, Anjaneyulu said, "Kneel, and each of you must touch your forehead to the ground."

When they had done this as well, he said: "Now stick your noses in the dung."

This, too, all of them did obediently. "Now raise your heads. Then count the number of noseprints in the cow dung," said Anjaneyulu like a patient teacher.

When Sowmayajulu and his disciples counted the number of noses in the cow dung, they were delighted to find that there were thirteen noses and not twelve!

"Our missing brother disciple has been found!" they all chorused. "We knew the city of Wisdom was near, and you who are so wise must be the gatekeeper!"

As they congratulated Anjaneyulu, who could barely keep himself from laughing out loud, they gave him all the worldly belongings they could afford. The thirteen seekers of Wisdom and Anjaneyulu in turn parted company, each satisfied with what he had found. But Anjaneyulu was the only one without cow dung on his face.

TREE GHOSTS AT NOON

Ghost stories form a great part of storytelling among children in India. When a monsoon strikes there are times, even in big cities, when there are power failures. At night, when the electricity goes off and plunges you into darkness, it is the perfect time to tell a ghost story.

In India, ghosts are commonly known as pichilipairi, meaning "reversed feet." Ghosts are also referred to as demons or rakshasa, even pisasi. It is a belief that the hot midday sun causes some ghosts to come out, and night with its glowing bright moon causes others to do so.

Tropical plains

Vast, dry grassland

Hot desert

Often grandmothers of south India will tell their grandchildren not to go out in the sun around noon. There are particular trees in which ghosts "hang out." One of them is the tamarind tree. So take care who you might meet there and talk to at that time!

The tamarind tree grows in tropical regions. Most of India has a tropical climate.

Meeting Mala

Josh stared after his cousins as they ran along the dusty road to school. This would be his first time alone since he came to visit them from England. But Josh wouldn't be stuck for things to do; there was lots to discover in this Chennai fishing village and he was dying to explore.

"Yippee!" Josh called. He looked up at the sun. It was high and hot in the cloudless sky. He could see the heat shimmer in silvery waves on the grass.

"Even with a hat, you mustn't go out at noon, Baba," Kuppu the caretaker had gently reasoned with him on the day of his arrival. "It's the heat. It can do funny things to you."

Josh looked at the casuarina trees to the right of the house. "Yes, that's it! If I said I went to explore the wildlife there, I'd be in no danger of the heat," he thought excitedly. He didn't want Kuppu to worry about him, so he left a note.

While Josh was in the grove, the sea air felt cool as the casuarina trees swayed with their feathery branches. Shafts of sunlight beamed down on him. He began turning cartwheels. "Yooohooo!" he shouted. No one answered. Suddenly he noticed a temple. But there were no flowers or lamps. He went around it. On the back stairs, there was a girl about his age.

"Hello!" she said, playing with her two braids, which were decorated with jasmine and bright yellow ribbons.

"Phew! You really frightened me," squeaked Josh. "I didn't think anyone was here."

"I study in that vikas. When there is a break, I go and fetch coconuts to sell to the vendor. The vendor didn't come so I came here to play." She stood up. Her pavadai skirt covered her feet. As she came toward Josh, he heard her anklets jingling.

"I'm Josh," he said, and dug his hands into his pockets as he shrugged his shoulders. "I'm exploring until my cousins come back from school."

"I'll teach you a few games then," she said, pulling out some cowrie shells. She swept the ground of bat droppings and dry leaves with the husks of coconuts lying close by. Her bangles tinkled. One of them broke and a glass chip, the color of blood, fell glinting in the sunlight.

She began in a low chant: "How-do-you-catch-the-demon?" With her right hand, she tossed Josh a cowrie to aim into her left hand, which had formed a cave on the ground. Her nails were long and stained with henna. "Catch the demon!" she shouted.

Josh aimed at the cave, but she slapped her hand flat before the cowrie got in. Josh caught on and tried aiming with the cowries she tossed him. "You lost! You lost!" She giggled and teased.

"Who's the demon?" Josh asked.

"Oh, the demon. He used to sing so badly that when he died, his spirit hung around the trees waiting to enter the body of a good singer. But no one came... Don't you know any games?" she asked sweetly.

"Er... yeah, but first I'll show you how we have a special greeting on our school playground." And Josh stretched out his hand. The girl did the same. Just then he heard "Baba! Baba!" That was Kuppu's voice.

"I'll be back," said Josh and ran in the direction of the voice. He turned around and asked: "What's your name?"

"Mala!" she said, clutching and wringing her pavadai.

He ran and found Kuppu in a sweat. "Baba! I told you not to come here by yourself."

"But Kuppu, I'm fine. Look, I met Mala and she's teaching me some games... and a bit of Tamil, too."

"Aiyiyo!" said Kuppu with despair. But Josh was pulling him to the ruined temple.

"Mala!" he shouted after the disappearing figure and the sound of anklets.

"There is no Mala," said Kuppu softly, but firmly.

"But she just played cowries with me here!" Josh pointed to the spot. It was covered with leaves and bat droppings.

"Baba, she is a spirit. She was a girl your age, many years ago. She wanted to be a singer and go to the city. We all told her it was not good. So, in the dead of night, she stood by the highway with the hope of getting a ride to the city. A speeding truck crushed her to death. Since then she's been looking for someone her age into whose body she can enter and use to go away from here."

"That must be someone else," said Josh, fighting his tears and Kuppu's story. "Look, this was a girl with red bangles. Here, one of them broke." As he searched among the leaves he only found bloodstains.

"Baba, at high noon, spirits of the dead come down from the trees to play games and trap the living. Let's go now," urged Kuppu gently.

Josh was shivering beneath the warmth of Kuppu's arm. What would have happened if his hand had touched Mala's, he wondered.

HUSBANDS AREN'T ✳ALWAYS RIGHT✳

This story from Kashmir was inspired by a collection of folk tales by the storyteller A. K. Ramanujan. It's a funny and unusual tale, possibly told to a woman before she marries to remind her that everything a husband says or does should not be accepted as law. It could be told during a ceremony before the wedding where only the bride and her female relatives are present.

It is very much a woman-centered tale passed down through the years from mothers to their daughters. It compares well with a trickster tale, where a person from a poorer background proves to be smarter than somebody who has all the advantages of education and wealth. In this story, the girl who becomes the wife of a wealthy merchant's son is from a poor ironsmith's family. Let's see who comes out on top in the end!

Kashmir is one of the most beautiful regions of India. It has lakes and the snow-capped mountains of the Himalayas.

The Wife Who Would Not Be Beaten

Once there lived a clever merchant and his loving wife. Their only son was lazy and stupid, and the merchant and his wife didn't know what to do with him. They decided to test him in the hope that he might try to use his mind a little. The merchant gave him four coins and said, "Go and buy something that will fill your stomach, quench your thirst, grows quickly and feeds the cow as well."

When the stupid son went to the market, he stood spellbound by all the noise. After eventually wasting three coins on useless goods, such as cotton candy and balloons, he decided to go for a walk.

The stupid son found it easier to speak his thoughts out loud than to think them in silence. So after he'd walked and thought for a while, many people knew about his test. Even so, the stupid son was surprised when suddenly a girl came up to him and said, "If you need to feed yourself, quench your thirst, grow something quickly, and feed the cow using the money your father has given you, then you need a watermelon."

The stupid son quickly did as she advised and set off to show the watermelon to his parents. The merchant said, "This must be someone else's idea."

When the son told him about the girl, an idea formed in the merchant's mind. "If my son marries this clever girl," he said, "she will keep him from looking so foolish."

The merchant found out where the girl lived, and went and asked her to marry his son. When the stupid son's friends heard why his father had gone to the poor ironsmith's house, they called their friend aside and said, "You can't marry a poor girl! Why don't you put off this marriage by telling the girl's father that you will beat her seven times a day with your leather slippers." The stupid son agreed.

On hearing this, the girl's father wanted her to call off the wedding. However, the girl only said, "Father, there is a big difference between what a man says he will do and what he actually does." Undaunted, she carried on with the wedding preparations.

On the wedding night, when the bride and groom were asleep, the stupid son awoke suddenly and raised his slipper to beat his wife. As she turned around, she calmly said, "Don't you know the custom? You must never beat your wife on the first night of marriage."

He nodded and fell back to sleep.

When he tried beating her the following night, she said, "Don't you know it is a bad omen to beat your wife in the first week of your marriage when the moon is full?"

So the stupid son waited. But, as was the custom for the girls in that village, the bride returned to her parents' home for a month on the eighth day after the marriage. Meanwhile, the stupid son decided to travel alone to distant lands and seek his fortune.

After two weeks of traveling, the stupid son came to a fort where a woman lived with many servants. She invited him to play a game. Her servants acted as game pieces, dressed in red for the woman and yellow for the stupid son. The servants had been ordered to help their mistress cheat. At the woman's signal, her cat would brush its bushy tail against the lamp, flashing its bright light into the stupid son's eyes. While he couldn't see, the servants changed their positions so that their mistress could win. The stupid son lost all his wealth and was thrown into prison where he met many other unfortunate, penniless men. There he was beaten and given very little food and water.

One day, the stupid son saw a man from his village ride past the prison window. He managed to give him letters for his father and his wife. As the rider could not read or write, the letters got mixed up. The merchant received the letter addressed to his daughter-in-law. It read, "I can't wait to return and beat you seven times a day." The wife received the letter addressed to her father-in-law that read: "I am treated so cruelly here, I doubt I'm ever coming out alive."

The stupid son's wife decided she would go and rescue him. Her father-in-law gave her money and servants. She disguised herself as a young, wealthy man. When she came to the fort, the wife, like all the unfortunate men before her, was invited by the woman to play a game.

However, the wife had bribed the servants with the merchant's money to tell her of their mistress's tricks. So when the time came to play the game, the disguised wife hid a mouse in her sleeve. Just when the cat began to brush its tail against the lamp, the wife let the mouse loose. The cat leaped out of its position to chase the mouse and completely forgot about its mistress. The wicked woman of the fort lost every game and all her riches.

The wife went down and released all the prisoners. Of course, her husband did not recognize her through her disguise. She told him to change into fresh clean clothes, while she took his ragged ones with her. The stupid son returned to his parents with all the wealth that his wife had won. The wife came to visit him and the first thing he said was, "Don't think I haven't forgotten. Get me my slippers. I will beat you now!"

"Stop! What kind of homecoming is this?" his parents shouted.

"What a mean person you are," his wife said. "After all that you have suffered with beatings and starvation, and then being saved, is that what you would want to do to another human being? I thought some sense would have been knocked into your head. I was the one who saved you. Here are your ragged clothes. I was the wealthy man who cheated her at her own game. You are too stupid to understand."

At this, the merchant and his wife said, "It's true, he is really stupid. We will give all our wealth to this girl who deserves it more, and let her do as she chooses." And that is how a poor, but clever, girl became a rich woman.

Glossary

Aiyiyo An exclamation of despair in Tamil.

Anklets Ankle bracelets worn by girls and women.

Baba The title of affection for boys in India.

Buk-buk Nonsense talk; clucking like a chicken.

Dhoti A cloth men wear around the waist folded like trousers.

Diwali Diwali, the festival of lights, symbolizes how good overcomes evil and how light dispels darkness. In the autumn it is also the Hindu New Year.

Henna An herb made into a paste that is used to paint nails and patterns on the palms of girls' hands, leaving a red dye stain.

Koyal The Indian nightingale.

Pavadai A long skirt that is gathered at the waist and covers the feet.

Red dot A mark of worship worn between the eyebrows by most married Hindu women. Hindu men also wear the mark on religious occasions.

Sati A practice in which a wife sits on the funeral pyre of her dead husband, so that she dies along with him. Banned in the nineteenth century, the practice still persists.

Tamarind A type of fruit tree that ghosts are fond of.

Tamil The language spoken by the people of Chennai.

Turmeric A root ground into a yellow powder. It is used in cooking, as an antiseptic, and it is worn in worship rituals.

Vikas Temple school.

Further Information

Books

Cumming, David. *India* (Country Insights). Austin, TX: Raintree Steck-Vaughn, 1998.

Hirst, Mike. *India* (Food and Festivals). Austin, TX: Raintree Steck-Vaughn, 1999.

Kagaa, Falaq. *India* (Festivals of the World). Milwaukee, WI: Gareth Stevens, Inc., 1997.

Kerven, Rosalind. *Id-ul-Fitr* (A World of Holidays). Austin, TX: Raintree Steck-Vaughn, 1997.

Lambert, David. *Asia*. (Continents.) Austin, TX: Raintree Steck-Vaughn, 1997.

Lerner Publications, Department of Geography Staff, ed. *India in Pictures*. (Visual Geography.) Minneapolis, MN: Lerner Publications, 1995.

McNair, Sylvia. *India*. (Enchantment of the World.) Danbury, CT: Children's Press, 1996.

Useful Addresses

Indian Embassy
2107 Massachusetts Avenue
Washington, DC 20008
202-939-7000

Indian Tourist Office
30 Rockefeller Plaza North
New York, NY 10112
212-586-4901

India Activities

Imagine you are the old woman in **Dead Man Walking**. Write your own song containing miracles that the baby will perform when she grows up. Then write the rest of the story based on these miracles.

Write the front-page story about **Valmiki** for a newspaper, detailing how the most feared highwayman in the region has become one of India's epic poets. Remember to start off with an eye-catching headline.

Imagine that you have accompanied **Tenali Rama** to Kali's temple and write about it afterward in your diary. Write about how you feel when you first confront the fearsome twenty-armed goddess. Then write about your realization when Rama points out the obvious.

Write **Folly's Wisdom** from Anjaneyulu's point of view: how he first saw the disciples, what he thought they were doing, and how he solved their problem.

Write a letter from Josh to his friend in England, telling him about the sights and sounds of India, and **Meeting Mala**. Finally, write part two of **The Wife Who Would Not Be Beaten**. What does the wife do with her new-found wealth?

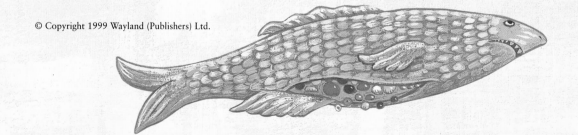